GW00670944

IPSWICH SPEEDWAY

A Decade
in Pictures

By Stephen Waller

First published in 2008 by
At Heart Ltd, 32 Stamford Street, Altrincham, Cheshire, WA14 1EY

in conjunction with
Evening Star, 30 Lower Brook Street, Ipswich, IP4 1AN

Text and images © 2008 Stephen Waller

All rights reserved. No part of this book may be reproduced in any
form or by any means, including information storage and retrieval
systems without permission in writing from the publisher, except
by a reviewer who may quote passages in a review.

ISBN: 978-1-84547-191-0

Printed and bound by: Ashford Colour Press, Gosport

About the author

Suffolk photographer Stephen Waller undertakes a wide range of photographic commissions in subjects ranging from weddings and portraits through to commercial, public relations and press work.

However, to many speedway fans it is for his sports photography that he is best known. As club photographer to Ipswich Witches, Stephen supplies images to the local and national press, including Ipswich's Evening Star, the club's main sponsor.

To view the full range of work covered by Stephen, including some of the many speedway meetings he has covered, visit his website at www.stephenwaller.com

About the club

Ipswich Witches have a long history as one of the country's best known speedway clubs. They race on most Thursday evenings during the summer months at Foxhall Stadium, on the outskirts of Ipswich. Fixtures and other information about the club can be viewed on their website at www.ipswich-witches.com

Acknowledgements

Thanks go to the riders, management and supporters of Ipswich Speedway for providing some great photographic opportunities over the years; to Dave Kindred for suggesting the concept of this book and for steering me in the right direction; and to club statistician Mike Smillie for his valuable input. Thanks also go to every publication which has taken my images over the years, and finally to my wife Elaine, who puts up with me working many long and often unsociable hours during my career as a photographer.

The 2008 Ipswich Witches

Preface

Photographer Stephen Waller has attended the majority of Ipswich Speedway meetings for more than a decade.

When Stephen started he was working with film. In more recent years as digital photography has taken over, he is a familiar sight on the centre green, working between races on his laptop computer as he transmits his photographs for the following day's newspapers.

Failing evening light, and often wet and cold conditions, all increase the challenge of a difficult, fast-moving subject, but Stephen always rises to the challenge.

Over the pages of this book he has selected more than 250 of his favourite images. We will see triumph and tribulation, both happy occasions and painful injury.

When Stephen started photographing at Foxhall Stadium, Ipswich Evening Star Witches were on top of the speedway world. In 1998 they won an amazing treble – the Elite League, the Knock-Out Cup and the Craven Shield. Major titles have eluded the club since and there have been some disappointing seasons, but it now looks like the Witches are set for better times.

Since they came into being in the early 1950s, Ipswich have had a chequered time. But what has shone through ever since the days when nearly 20,000 spectators used to crowd into Foxhall is the large fan base that the club enjoys. Perhaps it is the rural area, perhaps it is the East Anglian nature, but speedway fits into the spectrum of a great many Suffolk and north Essex folk.

Meetings at Foxhall now attract around 2,000 spectators, but it would not be an over-estimation to suggest that at least another 20,000 support the club away from the track. They either used to go, or are visitors for bank holidays and the odd Thursday meeting.

The club is lucky enough to have some of the most loyal supporters in the land; even when the chips are down Witches fans still turn up to witness the full-throttle action that the sport provides – enjoying watching the sport as much as their team does competing in it.

It is great to support a winning side, and I can still vividly recall the hundreds of Ipswich supporters who made their way to Reading to watch the British League title being won in 1984. Huge numbers ventured to venues like Coventry in 1998, and thousands paraded on the Cornhill when Ipswich were given a civic reception that year for winning the treble.

My association with the Witches goes back to the mid-50s, watching from the home straight stand as a keen-eyed lad in short trousers. In the mid-70s I was a regular on the back straight. Little did I realise then that from 1979, Foxhall would become an integral part of my life. When speedway correspondent Mike Horne left the Evening Star sports department I was handed the task of reporting on the Ipswich speedway team. I still take in every home Witches meeting and report on a large number.

A good speedway meeting beats any other sport for excitement, tension and thrills. I have travelled around the country for many years with Stephen and have been privileged enough to see him in action from close quarters. There are very few who can produce the same photographic results that Stephen does, and he is without doubt one of the very best in the business. Riders travel up to 65mph on machines with no brakes and there is no second chance to record the most spectacular incidents.

The lighting at most tracks leaves a lot to be desired, but you can depend on Stephen to come up with the shots that matter for the following day's *Evening Star*. It is fitting that he is putting his pictures into this book, and it will bring back a host of memories for Witches supporters. Most of the riders who have worn a Witches race jacket over the last decade are featured.

A downside of the sport is the crashes. While this can be agonising for riders like Mark Loram, who broke his leg at the start of the 2007 season, it provides some spectacular images for Stephen – as men and machines are contorted in ways that make dramatic viewing when snapped correctly.

I know from personal experience how difficult – and sensitive – the job can be.

Several years ago when Stephen was unavailable, the *Evening Star* armed me with a basic camera for a midweek trip to Hull. Taking action pictures was beyond my ability, and I did not even try. I took some pit shots and ventured on to the track when Jason Bunyan suffered a spill and was being treated on the ground for a thumb injury. As I ventured as close as I could to get a shot of the rider receiving treatment on the track, I was given a sharp reminder of the sensitivity of the photographer's job when Mr Bunyan senior let me know in no uncertain terms that I had taken a step too far. It would not have happened to Stephen, who would not only have had a longer lens, but would also have diplomatically got the picture that made the sports pages the following day.

They say that a picture is worth a thousand words and this portrayal of the Witches' recent past is well thought out, well designed, but most importantly, well photographed.

Take a look at your heroes – and perhaps villains – as they go through their paces putting their necks on the line to provide entertainment and thrills.

You can't beat being there, but this book is the next best thing. Enjoy.

Elvin King
Speedway correspondent, *Evening Star*

1998

1998 FINAL LEAGUE TABLE

	M	W	D	L	F	A	PTS	BP	TOT
IPSWICH	32	26	1	5	1653.5	1211.5	53	16	69
Belle Vue	32	20	0	12	1524.5	1353.5	40	12	52
Coventry	32	18	1	13	1474.0	1401.0	37	11	48
Swindon	32	15	1	16	1429.0	1450.0	31	7	38
Eastbourne	32	15	0	17	1430.0	1449.0	30	7	37
Wolverhampton	32	14	1	17	1421.0	1444.0	29	8	37
Oxford	32	13	2	17	1388.0	1490.0	28	5	33
Poole	32	11	1	20	1348.0	1529.0	23	5	28
King's Lynn	32	8	1	23	1270.0	1610.0	17	1	18

The 1998 all conquering Ipswich Witches with the KOC trophy. From left to right: Tomasz Gollob, Toni Svab, Tony Rickardsson, John Louis (promoter), Scott Nicholls, Savalas Clouting and Chris Louis.

With a heat leader trio of Tomasz Gollob (below left), Tony Rickardsson and Chris Louis (left) – all leading Grand Prix riders at the time – the Witches promotion had assembled a potent spearhead for the 1998 side.

Witches promoter John Louis with the Craven Shield.

Tony Rickardsson turns on the style during press day in 1998.

Scott Nicholls and Chris Louis lead Mikael Karlsson and Garry Stead at Wolverhampton.

Craig Boyce (right) challenges Tony Rickardsson at Poole.

Tomasz Gollob charges across Poole's Mark Lemon and Craig Boyce to join team-mate Chris Louis.

Scott Nicholls (left) and Toni Svab lead Gary Havelock and Magnus Zetterstrom.

Chris Louis puts an inside move on Joe Screen (centre) during the meeting, helping him secure the first British title of his career.

Chris had great support from the Witches fans on the terraces (top). Here he is celebrating with fans after winning the title.

BRITISH 98
FINAL
B.S.P.A.

Chris Louis on the rostrum alongside Joe Screen (left) and Paul Hurry. Below left, he is given the bumps by his pit crew after securing the title.

Chris is congratulated by his father John, who also won the crown in 1975.

Ipswich's Savalas Clouting also rode in the 1998 British Final. After starting the meeting in fine form he was involved in this frightening crash with Joe Screen.

A tight first bend at Foxhall in a meeting against the Eastbourne Eagles, in which David Norris falls between Tony Rickardsson (left) and Chris Louis. Gary Havelock is the Eagles rider on the right.

Tony Rickardsson (left) and Chris Louis congratulate each other after another maximum heat win.

Look no hands! Tomasz Gollob celebrates on his way back to the pits after a race win at Coventry.

It's a dirty job: Chris Louis was virtually unrecognisable after getting covered in shale during a local derby meeting at King's Lynn during the '98 season.

Tomasz Gollob (left) and Tony Rickardsson celebrate with the Witches fans after securing a 5-1 match winning victory in the final heat at Eastbourne.

All smiles from Savalas Clouting (left) and Scott Nicholls on the Eastbourne tractor.

Scott Nicholls holds off the challenge of King's Lynn's Shane Parker at Foxhall.

Rickardsson, Gollob and Louis were all competing at the top of the Grand Prix series in 1998. Here Jason Crump celebrates on the top of the rostrum at the British Grand Prix at Coventy, with Jimmy Nilsen (left) and Gollob (right).

Tony Rickardsson in Grand Prix action.

Chris Louis chases eventual winner Jason Crump in the Grand Prix.

You couldn't mistake the Witches supporters at Coventry.

Tony Rickardsson celebrates with John Louis after securing the 1998 league title.

Savalas Clouting gives Tony Rickardsson a lift as the riders walk the track on a victory parade.

Tony Rickardsson with long time Witches supporter Ruby Woods, who is otherwise known as 'Mum Witch'.

The team with the Craven Shield trophy after winning their third title at Coventry.

Tomasz Gollob, Toni Svab, Tony Rickardsson, Chris Louis, Savalas Clouting and Scott Nicholls with the Elite League Trophy.

The Witches enjoyed great support on the terraces away from home during the 1998 season.

Fans turned out in force when the club was awarded a civic reception in honour of their treble winning achievements.

The team are pictured inside the Town Hall with Mayor Hamill Clarke MBE and his wife Grace.

Tony Rickardsson also tasted success on an individual level with victory in the Grand Prix series. In honour of his world championship, he and his pit crew were paraded around the Ipswich track in a horse-drawn carriage.

1998 RIDER AVERAGES – ALL OFFICIAL MATCHES (LEAGUE, CUP & CRAVEN SHIELD)

	M	R	PTS	BP	TOT	CMA	F	P
Tony Rickardsson	46	255	618.5	41	659.5	10.35	3	9
Tomasz Gollob	43	241	536	29	565	9.38	3	1
Chris Louis	45	252	522	67	589	9.35	1	5
Scott Nicholls	44	222	298	58	356	6.41	0	0
Toni Svab	45	191	195	43	238	4.98	0	0
Savalas Clouting	45	190	167	32	199	4.19	0	0

1999 FINAL LEAGUE TABLE

	M	W	D	L	F	A	PTS	BP	TOT
Peterborough	18	12	2	4	889.0	734.0	26	8	34
Poole	18	12	0	6	899.0	724.0	24	9	33
King's Lynn	18	11	1	6	823.0	804.0	23	6	29
Coventry	18	11	1	6	821.0	804.0	23	5	28
IPSWICH	18	11	0	7	815.0	810.0	22	4	26
Belle Vue	18	9	1	8	848.0	773.0	19	5	24
Hull	18	6	1	11	785.0	834.0	13	3	16
Oxford	18	5	0	13	754.0	869.0	10	3	13
Eastbourne	18	6	0	12	745.0	879.0	12	1	13
Wolverhampton	18	4	0	14	736.0	884.0	8	1	9

The 1999 Ipswich Witches: (from left to right) Jason Bunyan, Brett Woodifield, team manager Mike Smillie, Chris Louis, Savalas Clouting, Tomasz Gollob, Ben Howe and Toni Svab.

Rickardsson and co-promoter Mike Western (pictured left) moved to King's Lynn amid a certain amount of bad feeling ahead of the 1999 season, and when Ipswich arrived for their Good Friday fixture they found a number of pyrotechnic witches on the centre green.

The Lynn mike man announced that one was to be blown up with each 5-1 the home side scored. However with the Witches providing more resistance than Lynn perhaps expected, the home side had to find lesser reasons to explode the Witches as the meeting progressed.

When Ipswich returned for their next visit, King's Lynn had brought in Leigh Adams to strengthen their side. Here Chris Louis is seen leading Adams during that meeting.

Savalas Clouting (nearest the camera), Mario Jirout, Chris Louis and
Jason Crump leave the start in the opening heat of Ipswich's Elite
League clash against Peterborough at Foxhall.

The Ipswich team is interviewed in the trackside Sky Sports studio at the end of a televised league meeting against Eastbourne.

Tomasz Gollob comes to grief after contact with Sam Ermolenko.

Tomasz Gollob celebrating a race victory at Foxhall.

Ready for the off: Chris Louis concentrates at the tapes.

Flat out: Chris Louis and Mark Loram race for the finish at Poole.

Brett Woodifield and Jason Bunyan ahead of Belle Vue's Phil Morris.

Team riding: Toni Svab (left) and Ben Howe keep out Charlie Gjedde.

Toni Svab (right) leaves the tapes alongside Todd Wiltshire at Oxford.

Savalas Clouting gets showered in shale as he chases Jesper B. Jensen in the opening heat of a match at Wolverhampton.

Tomasz Gollob taking it easy in the pits at King's Lynn.

1999 RIDER AVERAGES – ALL OFFICIAL MATCHES
(LEAGUE, CUP & CRAVEN SHIELD)

	M	R	PTS	BP	TOT	CMA	F	P
Tomasz Gollob	35	178	397	14	411	9.24	4	2
Chris Louis	39	196	404	35	439	8.96	0	4
Toni Svab	38	176	297	24	321	7.30	0	0
Ben Howe	12	48	63	13	76	6.33	0	0
Tomas Topinka	24	103	135	28	163	6.33	0	0
Savalas Clouting	38	150	161	26	187	4.99	0	1
Brett Woodifield	40	170	175	30	205	4.82	0	0
Jason Bunyan	29	99	62	21	83	3.35	0	0
David Osborn	1	3	0	0	0	0.00	0	0

2000 FINAL LEAGUE TABLE

	M	W	D	L	F	A	PTS	BP	TOT
Eastbourne	32	24	1	7	1544.0	1322.0	49	13	62
King's Lynn	32	22	2	8	1564.0	1321.0	46	14	60
IPSWICH	32	16	3	13	1456.5	1409.5	35	11	46
Coventry	32	16	3	13	1442.0	1427.0	35	8	43
Poole	32	14	4	14	1437.0	1426.0	32	8	40
Wolverhampton	32	15	3	14	1396.0	1467.0	33	6	39
Peterborough	32	11	2	19	1431.5	1425.5	24	7	31
Oxford	32	9	1	21	1296.0	1477.0	19	4	23
Belle Vue	32	5	3	23	1249.0	1541.0	13	1	14

The Ipswich Witches team in 2000. Back row, from the left: Toni Svab, team manager Mike Smillie, Chris Louis, Matej Ferjan, Jason Bunyan and Tomasz Gollob. Front row: Savalas Clouting and Lawrence Hare.

A big wheelie from Chris Louis at press day 2000.

Jason Bunyan inside Andre Compton.

Lawrence Hare celebrates a race victory.

Pole Jarek Hampel wishes he'd made the start in the atrocious conditions during a meeting at Peterborough, but still finds something to smile about.

Lawrence Hare and Jason Bunyan lead Steve Masters at King's Lynn as the riders struggle to see through the driving rain.

Speedway Control Board referee Chris Gay discusses track conditions with riders as the rains come down at Foxhall.

Tomasz Gollob celebrates a
race success...

...while things don't look to have gone so well
for Witches skipper Chris Louis.

Toni Svab up at the tapes and ready for lift off.

Matej Ferjan on a lap of honour at Foxhall
after being crowned Continental Champion
a few days earlier.

Deep in thought: Tomasz Gollob
relaxes in the pits.

John Louis congratulates Jason Bunyan
at Belle Vue after the youngster's
top score helps the Witches secure a
narrow win against the Aces.

Witches sponsor, the late Tim Woodward,
on the centre green at Foxhall with Ipswich
promoter John Louis.

Just three weeks after top scoring at Belle Vue, Jason Bunyan's season was over after a frightening crash in a live televised meeting at Wolverhampton. In difficult conditions he got tangled with Wolves' Sam Ermolenko going down the straight, and the pair smashed through the first bend fence at full speed. The Ipswich rider suffered a broken leg as a result.

Lawrence Hare received a broken wrist in this crash at Poole. Emil Lindqvist is the rider about to run over Hare, while Jeremy Doncaster is the fallen Witch behind.

Witches star Chris Louis (far right) was able to walk away from this heavy fall in the British Grand Prix. Swedes Peter Karlsson (left) and Stefan Danno are the other riders involved.

Ipswich's Polish star, Tomasz Gollob.

2000 RIDER AVERAGES – ALL OFFICIAL MATCHES
(LEAGUE, CUP & CRAVEN SHIELD)

	M	R	PTS	BP	TOT	CMA	F	P
Chris Louis	34	173	389	25	414	9.57	2	6
Tomasz Gollob	21	113	259	10	269	9.52	1	0
Matej Ferjan	36	163	242	24	266	6.53	0	0
Toni Svab	37	167	244	28	272	6.51	0	0
Jeremy Doncaster	30	141	193	23	216	6.13	0	0
Jarek Hampel	3	15	16	4	20	5.33	0	0
Jason Bunyan	19	71	65.5	17	82.5	4.65	0	0
Savalas Clouting	7	27	27	1	28	4.15	0	0
Lawrence Hare	25	82	56	16	72	3.51	0	0
Jan Andersen	14	52	35	10	45	3.46	0	0
James Mann	1	3	0	0	0	0.00	0	0
David Osborn	2	6	0	0	0	0.00	0	0

2001 FINAL LEAGUE TABLE

	M	W	D	L	F	A	PTS	BP	TOT
Oxford	32	20	5	7	1495.0	1367.0	45	13	58
Poole	32	21	2	9	1538.0	1325.0	44	13	57
Coventry	32	21	2	9	1518.0	1356.0	44	11	55
IPSWICH	32	17	2	13	1444.0	1429.0	36	7	43
Peterborough	30	12	2	16	1356.0	1329.0	26	7	33
King's Lynn	32	12	1	19	1381.0	1467.0	25	7	32
Eastbourne	32	11	3	18	1373.0	1463.0	25	7	32
Wolverhampton	32	12	0	20	1397.0	1478.0	24	4	28
Belle Vue	30	7	1	22	1196.0	1484.0	15	1	16

* Peterborough & Belle Vue did not complete their fixtures.

The 2001 Ipswich Witches: (from the left) Scott Nicholls, Craig Boyce, Jason Bunyan, Chris Louis, Savalas Clouting, Jarek Hampel and Jeremy Doncaster.

Australian Craig Boyce who joined the club in 2001.

Craig Boyce on the inside of Tony Rickardsson at Poole.

Chris Louis just gets his nose ahead of Poole's Gary Havelock at Wimborne Road.

Former riders Charlie Frenzel (front left), Titch Read (front centre), Bert Edwards (front right), Derek Hewitt (back left) and Rod Laudrum (back right) are given a lap of honour at the Witches' 50th anniversary meeting.

Former stars: Bert Edwards talks with promoter John Louis.

Former Witches team-mates Tony Davey and John Louis took part in a match race at the anniversary meeting.

Louis gets his breath back after the race.

Jeremy Doncaster leading David Norris at Eastbourne.

Savalas Clouting leads Steve Johnston, Marcus Andersson and team-mate Jason Bunyan during the same meeting.

Jeremy Doncaster chats to Sky Sports' Suzi
Perry in the Eastbourne pits.

Jarek Hampel is the meat in the Californian sandwich provided by
Coventry riders Billy Janniro (left) and Billy Hamill.

Ipswich staged a test match between Great Britain and Australia at Foxhall in 2001, with Chris Louis riding for Team GB and Craig Boyce competing for the Aussies. Lining up for Great Britain are (from left to right): Carl Stonehewer, Gary Havelock, Mark Loram, Chris Louis (on bike) Neil Middleditch (team manager), Paul Hurry, Scott Nicholls and David Howe.

For Australia (from left to right): Jason Crump, Leigh Adams, Steve Johnston, Craig Boyce, Todd Wiltshire, Ryan Sullivan and Shane Parker.

Todd Wiltshire leads Chris Louis during the Test.

Craig Boyce was presented with an award for his contribution to Australian sport during a meeting between Ipswich and King's Lynn. Lynn's Jason Crump also received an award, and the pair are pictured with Australian team manager, Neil Street.

Jarek Hampel at work on his machine in the Witches' pits.

2001 RIDER AVERAGES – ALL OFFICIAL MATCHES (LEAGUE, CUP & CRAVEN SHIELD)

	M	R	PTS	BP	TOT	CMA	F	P
Scott Nicholls	37	184	446	19	465	10.11	6	3
Craig Boyce	41	200	382	21	403	8.06	0	0
Chris Louis	32	152	263	33	296	7.79	2	0
Jarek Hampel	40	192	310	43	353	7.35	0	1
Jeremy Doncaster	44	184	254	38	292	6.35	0	1
Jason Bunyan	43	161	86	21	107	2.66	0	0
Savalas Clouting	40	150	72	6	78	2.08	0	0
Carl Baldwin	3	9	2	0	2	0.89	0	0

2002 FINAL LEAGUE TABLE

	M	W	D	L	F	A	PTS	BP	TOT
Eastbourne	32	20	3	9	1562.0	1316.0	43	15	58
Wolverhampton	32	20	2	10	1548.0	1311.0	42	12	54
Coventry	32	19	3	10	1492.0	1383.0	41	9	50
Poole	32	17	1	14	1455.0	1406.0	35	11	46
Peterborough	31	15	0	16	1394.0	1395.0	30	7	37
Oxford	31	14	2	15	1369.0	1407.0	30	5	35
IPSWICH	32	11	3	18	1375.0	1494.0	25	5	30
Belle Vue	32	11	3	18	1379.0	1484.0	25	4	29
King's Lynn	32	7	1	24	1247.0	1625.0	15	3	18

* Peterborough & Oxford did not complete their fixtures.

The 2002 Ipswich Witches team. From the left: Scott Nicholls, Carl Baldwin, Chris Louis, Jeremy Doncaster, Leigh Lanham, Craig Boyce (kneeling), Danny Bird and Joonas Kylmakorpi.

Leigh Lanham at press day.

Tony Rickardsson and Craig Boyce battle for the lead
at Poole with Jarek Hampel just behind.

Scott Nicholls ahead of Piotr Protasiewicz at
Peterborough's East of England showground.

Chris Louis

Craig Boyce leading Savalas Clouting at Eastbourne.

Jeremy Doncaster (left) and
Joe Screen race from the
start at Eastbourne.

Scott Nicholls (right)
welcomes Kim Jansson to
the club towards the end
of the season.

2002 British Champion, Scott Nicholls.

2002 RIDER AVERAGES – ALL OFFICIAL MATCHES
(LEAGUE, CUP & CRAVEN SHIELD)

	M	R	PTS	BP	TOT	CMA	F	P
Scott Nicholls	36	194	455	17	472	9.73	0	3
Jarek Hampel	19	96	171	16	187	7.79	0	0
Craig Boyce	40	190	309	27	336	7.07	1	1
Chris Louis	10	51	77	6	83	6.51	0	0
Chris Slabon	26	123	158	32	190	6.18	0	0
Jeremy Doncaster	30	120	125	28	153	5.10	0	0
Danny Bird	18	76	80	16	96	5.05	0	0
Joonas Kylmakorpi	33	130	139	23	162	4.98	0	0
Kim Jansson	8	29	23	6	29	4.00	0	0
Leigh Lanham	21	80	65	13	78	3.90	0	0
Carl Baldwin	5	15	2	1	3	0.80	0	0

2003 FINAL LEAGUE TABLE

	M	W	D	L	F	A	PTS	BP	TOT
Poole	28	20	1	7	1335.0	1182.0	41	11	52
Coventry	28	17	0	11	1295.0	1224.0	34	10	44
Peterborough	28	16	0	12	1325.0	1195.0	32	8	40
Oxford	28	16	0	12	1295.0	1224.0	32	8	40
Wolverhampton	28	14	1	13	1248.0	1265.0	29	6	35
Eastbourne	28	12	1	15	1261.0	1250.0	25	8	33
Belle Vue	28	9	1	18	1219.0	1298.0	19	5	24
IPSWICH	28	6	0	22	1088.0	1428.0	12	0	12

The 2003 Ipswich Witches: (from the left) Daniel Nermark, Paul Hurry, Chris Slabon, Scott Nicholls, Jarek Hampel, Tom P. Madsen, Mike Smillie (team manager) and Danny Bird.

Team-mates Daniel Nermark and Daniel King crashed spectacularly at King's Lynn in a British League Cup meeting.

Daniel Nermark ahead of Joe Screen.

Scott Nicholls retained his
British Championship.

Tom P. Madsen (left) and Daniel King talk tactics.

Kim Jansson drops the clutch.

Daniel Nermark and Henning Bager were both grateful for the Arena Essex air fence, which saved them from serious injury in this high-speed crash.

Not much room between Paul Hurry (left) and Charlie Gjedde, as they battle for the lead at Oxford.

2003 RIDER AVERAGES – ALL OFFICIAL MATCHES
(LEAGUE, CUP, BL CUP & CRAVEN SHIELD)

	M	R	PTS	BP	TOT	CMA	F	P
Scott Nicholls	29	165	376	12	388	9.41	1	1
Jarek Hampel	18	95	142	13	155	6.53	0	0
Kim Jansson	13	57	74	18	92	6.46	0	0
Chris Slabon	23	110	142	21	163	5.93	0	0
Danny Bird	21	81	113	7	120	5.93	0	0
Paul Hurry	25	111	146	18	164	5.91	0	0
Daniel Nermark	37	170	216	22	238	5.60	0	0
Daniel King	8	38	47	5	52	5.47	0	0
Leigh Lanham	12	53	57	7	64	4.83	0	0
Tom P. Madsen	21	80	77	17	94	4.70	0	0
Freddie Eriksson	14	58	47	12	59	4.07	0	0
Craig Boyce	8	38	32	6	38	4.00	0	0
Ben Howe	6	20	15	4	19	3.80	0	0
Matthew Wright	3	9	2	0	2	0.89	0	0
Carl Baldwin	1	3	0	0	0	0.00	0	0

2004 FINAL LEAGUE TABLE

	M	W	D	L	F	A	PTS	BP	TOT
Poole	36	23	2	11	1721.0	1603.0	48	13	61
Wolverhampton	36	21	0	15	1729.0	1586.0	42	16	58
IPSWICH	36	21	0	15	1701.0	1626.0	42	11	53
Eastbourne	36	18	3	15	1699.0	1632.0	39	11	50
Oxford	36	19	0	17	1679.0	1672.0	38	10	48
Swindon	36	18	3	15	1657.0	1667.0	39	6	45
Belle Vue	35	17	0	18	1630.0	1597.0	34	9	43
Arena Essex	36	16	0	20	1651.0	1679.0	32	8	40
Peterborough	35	12	2	21	1514.0	1722.0	26	2	28
Coventry	36	9	0	27	1565.0	1762.0	18	3	21

* Peterborough & Belle Vue did not complete their fixtures.

The 2004 Ipswich Witches: (from the left) Daniel King, Jesper B. Jensen, Kim Jansson, Hans Andersen, Scott Nicholls, Jan Staechmann, Danny Bird, Chris Louis and team manager Mike Smillie.

New Witches signing Hans Andersen shows his style with a press day wheelie.

Hans Andersen

Jesper B. Jensen

Kim Jansson

Action from the 2004 British Grand Prix at the Millennium Stadium, Cardiff. Chris Louis soaks up the atmosphere on the pre-meeting parade (left), while Scott Nicholls leads the way from Piotr Protasiewicz (above).

Hans Andersen with the Scandinavian
Grand Prix trophy.

Chris Louis makes some adjustments to
his machine.

Arena Essex rider Leigh Lanham takes the chequered flag in heat 2 of the Witches' clash against the
Hammers as a torrential downpour arrives.

A spectacular crash, as the Witches' Daniel King (blue helmet) gets caught up with Belle Vue's Kenneth Bjerre (yellow) and Joe Screen (green) after a tight first corner. Jesper B. Jensen is the Ipswich rider on the inside, who manages to stay out of trouble.

Swindon's Glenn Cunningham takes a tumble after running into Daniel King at Blunsdon.

Hans Andersen and Leigh Richardson battle at Peterborough.

Put it there: Danny Bird (left) and Kim Jansson
celebrate a maximum heat win at Foxhall.

Kim Jansson

A Scott Nicholls wheelie.

Scott Nicholls enjoyed fine weather when his testimonial was staged at Foxhall Stadium in 2004.

Joker Shane Parker cools down meeting presenter Kevin Long at Nicholls' testimonial.

Ipswich qualified for the 2004 play-offs and took Wolverhampton to a run-off in their semi-final clash against the Wolves at Monmore Green. Hans Andersen was the man to go up against Wolves' Mickael Karlsson (below) but lost out and looked dejected in the pits afterwards (left).

The Witches also reached the final of the Knock Out Cup, where they finished as runners up. Here Hans Andersen leads the way in front of Krzysztof Kasprzak and Bjarne Pedersen in the opening heat at Poole.

The Witches riders and management are pictured with their runner-up trophies.

Jesper B. Jensen ahead of Jason Lyons and team-mate Chris Louis.

2004 RIDERS AVERAGES – ALL OFFICIAL MATCHES
(LEAGUE, CUP & CRAVEN SHIELD)

	M	R	PTS	BP	TOT	CMA	F	P
Scott Nicholls	39	189	419	22	441	9.33	1	3
Hans Andersen	41	195	399	20	419	8.59	0	1
Chris Louis	44	193	366	34	400	8.29	0	1
Jesper B. Jensen	39	172	277	37	314	7.30	0	1
Danny Bird	25	106	148	24	172	6.49	0	0
Kim Jansson	44	204	243	61	304	5.96	0	0
Paul Pickering	6	24	21	4	25	4.17	0	0
Daniel King	44	171	123	18	141	3.30	0	0
Trevor Harding	10	34	10	2	12	1.41	0	0
Tom Brown	1	3	0	0	0	0.00	0	0

2005 FINAL LEAGUE TABLE

	M	W	D	L	F	A	PTS	BP	TOT
Belle Vue	36	24	0	12	1766.0	1520.0	48	13	61
Coventry	36	23	0	13	1739.0	1605.0	46	13	59
Peterborough	36	21	2	13	1709.0	1598.0	44	12	56
Eastbourne	36	19	1	16	1658.0	1646.0	39	10	49
Poole	36	18	1	17	1666.0	1647.0	37	10	47
IPSWICH	36	16	3	17	1661.0	1672.0	35	9	44
Swindon	36	17	2	17	1617.0	1675.0	36	7	43
Wolverhampton	36	14	2	20	1682.0	1647.0	30	10	40
Oxford	36	11	1	24	1550.0	1773.0	23	3	26
Arena Essex	36	11	0	25	1539.0	1804.0	22	3	25

Ipswich Witches, 2005: (from the left) team manager Mike Smillie, Daniel King, Karol Baran, Hans Andersen, Kevin Doolan, Chris Louis, Robert Miskowiak, Piotr Protasiewicz, Kim Jansson and promoter John Louis.

Shoulder to shoulder: Daniel King (right) battles with Steve Boxall during heat 6 of the British Under-21 Final at Rye House.

Chris Louis and Hans Andersen relive a tight first corner in the Eastbourne pits after racing to a final heat maximum over the Eagles' Nicki Pedersen and David Norris.

Daniel King races through water as he leads Edward Kennett.

Kim Jansson goes head first into the Arena Essex air fence.

Kevin Doolan (green helmet) suffered a broken arm in this heavy fall at Swindon, after a tight first corner with team-mate Robert Miskowiak and Swindon's Seb Tresarrieu.

Former Witches star Jeremy Doncaster had his farewell meeting at Foxhall in 2005. Here he is pictured with his old team-mate Armando Castagna.

Trials rider Jeff Hibbs entertains the fans during the interval by jumping his machine over a number of the riders.

Winner of the Jeremy Doncaster farewell meeting, Jason Crump, together with runner up, Scott Nicholls (left), and third-placed Leigh Lanham.

Jason Crump shows his support with a Jeremy Doncaster rosette.

Jeremy Doncaster (outside) in action against Armando Castagna during a match race between the two former team-mates.

Pictured with Doncaster (centre) are John Richardson, Mick Banthorpe, June Allum and David Hardiman, who brought a new dimension to the starting gates by dressing as cleaning ladies for this meeting.

Robert Miskowiak suffered no serious damage after cartwheeling over the fence in a televised league meeting at Sandy Lane, Oxford.

Piotr Protasiewicz in trouble on the inside of Charlie Gjedde at Swindon.

Chris Louis is interviewed by Sky Sports' Sophie Blake.

Half power: Foxhall Stadium in semi-darkness with only a few of the stadium floodlights switched on after a power failure.

Chris Louis (right) welcomes new signing Marius Puszakowski to the club.

Mariusz Puszakowski celebrates a successful meeting by sharing his man of the match champagne with the supporters.

2005 RIDERS AVERAGES – ALL OFFICIAL MATCHES (LEAGUE, CUP & CRAVEN SHIELD)

	M	R	PTS	BP	TOT	CMA	F	P
Hans Andersen	38	189	409	37	446	9.44	1	4
Chris Louis	32	138	265	26	291	8.43	0	2
Piotr Protasiewicz	37	169	319	15	334	7.91	1	2
Robert Miskowiak	40	194	298	41	339	6.99	0	0
Kim Jansson	38	161	214	24	238	5.91	0	0
Daniel King	31	132	106	20	126	3.82	0	0
Kevin Doolan	10	39	28	4	32	3.28	0	0
Karol Baran	24	90	58	13	71	3.16	0	0
Mariusz Puszakowski	5	22	28	1	29	5.27	0	0
George Stancl	4	18	24	3	27	6.00	0	0
Carl Wilkinson	3	15	12	0	12	3.20	0	0

2006 FINAL LEAGUE TABLE

	M	W	D	L	F	A	PTS	BP	TOT
Peterboorough	40	24	0	16	1942.0	1731.0	48	16	64
Reading	40	25	1	14	1934.0	1756.0	51	13	64
Swindon	40	23	1	16	1893.0	1786.0	47	14	61
Coventry	40	23	1	16	1861.0	1835.0	47	11	58
Belle Vue	40	21	0	19	1880.0	1761.0	42	15	57
Wolverhampton	40	20	2	18	1827.0	1840.0	42	10	52
Poole	40	19	0	21	1880.0	1811.0	38	13	51
IPSWICH	40	19	0	21	1847.0	1837.0	38	8	46
Eastbourne	40	20	1	19	1791.0	1860.0	41	5	46
Oxford	40	12	0	28	1696.0	1989.0	24	2	26
Arena Essex	40	11	0	29	1658.0	2003.0	22	3	25

Ipswich Witches 2006: (from the left) Kim Jansson, Chris Louis, Carl Wilkinson, Daniel King, Piotr Protasiewicz, Mark Loram, Steve Boxall, Jan Jaros, Robert Miskowiak and mascot Brendon Warvill.

Team-mates Robert Miskowiak (yellow helmet) and Piotr Protasiewicz get it all wrong during a Suffolk Cup meeting against near neighbours Mildenhall, but both are able to walk away.

"Hey you!": Kim Jansson plays up to the camera.

Chris Louis on a charge.

Daniel King (blue helmet) takes a trip over the air fence
after colliding with Coventry's Rory Schlein.

Mark Loram (left) and team manager Mike Smillie talk tactics.

Piotr Protasiewicz and Daniel King lead Brent Werner at Arena Essex.

Piotr Protasiewicz (red), Hans Andersen (green) and Ulrich Ostergaard (yellow) battle during a Foxhall clash between the Ipswich Witches and Peterborough Panthers.

Jan Jaros crashes out on the outside of Scott Nicholls.

Piotr Protasiewicz does the splits as he clashes with Shaun Tacey.

Kim Jansson chases Edward Kennett.

Chris Louis celebrates.

Chris Louis is interviewed by Sky Sports' Jonathan Green (left) and Kelvin Tatum.

German Tobi Kroner is welcomed to Ipswich by skipper Chris Louis.

Digging in: Poles Robert Miskowiak (left) and Piotr Protasiewicz check out the starting grids.

Kim Jansson in action.

Robert Miskowiak leading Joonas Kylmakorpi.

Not much room here between Coventry's Billy Janniro (left) and Rory Schlein (centre), and the Witches' Mark Loram in this Foxhall clash between Ipswich and Coventry.

Loram leads the way from Leigh Lanham (green helmet), Steve Johnston (yellow) and Danny King (blue).

Chris Louis holds off Scott Nicholls at Lakeside.

Piotr Protasiewicz leads Swindon's Leigh Adams.

Piotr Protasiewicz comes close to hitting the Foxhall fence.

Kim Jansson and Mark Loram battle with Belle Vue's Joe Screen (green helmet) and Jason Crump.

Robert Miskowiak and Chris Louis congratulate each other on a maximum heat win.

2006 RIDERS AVERAGES – ALL OFFICIAL MATCHES
(LEAGUE, CUP & CRAVEN SHIELD)

	M	R	PTS	BP	TOT	CMA	F	P
Mark Loram	42	209	458	8	466	8.92	0	0
Piotr Protasiewicz	36	164	312	20	332	8.10	0	1
Chris Louis	35	166	301	32	333	8.02	1	2
Kim Jansson	41	176	239	47	286	6.50	0	0
Robert Miskowiak	40	175	253	30	283	6.47	0	1
Daniel King	30	139	154	40	194	5.58	0	0
Carl Wilkinson	11	45	37	9	46	4.09	0	0
Tobias Kroner	21	85	61	16	77	3.62	0	0
Jan Jaros	18	71	44	9	53	2.99	0	0
Steve Boxall	2	9	9	1	10	4.44	0	0

2007 FINAL LEAGUE TABLE

	M	W	D	L	F	A	PTS	BP	TOT
Coventry	36	28	1	7	1819.0	1463.0	57	16	73
Swindon	36	26	1	9	1853.5	1451.5	53	14	67
Peterborough	36	25	1	10	1757.0	1501.0	51	12	63
Poole	36	22	1	13	1761.0	1514.0	45	13	58
Arena Essex/Lakeside	36	16	2	18	1605.0	1690.0	34	8	42
Wolverhampton	36	16	1	19	1602.0	1685.0	33	8	41
Eastbourne	36	12	2	22	1624.5	1676.5	26	7	33
Reading	36	11	1	24	1497.0	1779.0	23	3	26
IPSWICH	36	9	2	25	1464.0	1809.0	20	5	25
Belle Vue	36	9	0	27	1439.0	1853.0	18	4	22

The 2007 Ipswich Witches. Back row, from the left: Robert Miskowiak, Chris Schramm, Zibi Suchecki, Chris Louis (on bike), Tobi Kroner, Marcin Rempala and team mascot Brendon Warvill. Kneeling: Kim Jansson (left) and Mark Loram.

Tobi Kroner takes off.

Kim Jansson gets ready for a start...

...and celebrates a victory.

The Witches' hopes for a good season were over almost before it began when No.1, Mark Loram, was seriously injured in the first heat of the very first league meeting of the season. The former World champion was about to pass Reading's Sam Simota on the outside when the pair crashed through the fence, leaving Loram with a badly broken left leg.

Medics tend to the injured riders.

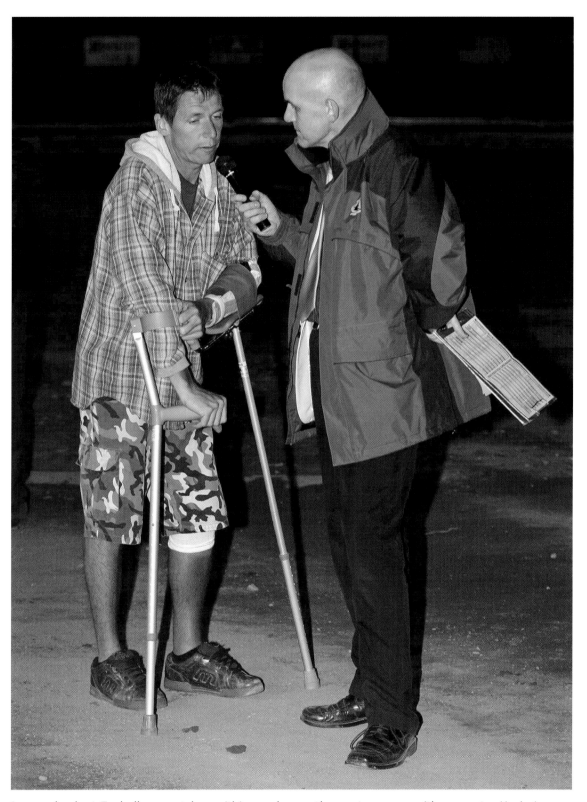

Loram, back at Foxhall on crutches within weeks, on the centre green with presenter Kevin Long.

Robert Miskowiak celebrates a good performance.

Tobi Kroner leading Danny King and Richard Hall of Peterborough.

Kim Jansson holds off Billy Janniro of Coventry.

Marcin Rempala inside Lakeside's Christian Hefenbrock.

Thumbs up from Robert Miskowiak.

An impressive Miskowiak wheelie.

Chris Louis

Marcin Rempala about to drop the clutch.

Zibi Suchecki leading Henning Bager at Lakeside.

Marcin Rempala loses control and crashes spectacularly in a meeting against Lakeside at Foxhall.

Former Witches rider Lawrence Hare, who is now confined to a wheelchair after a track crash at Newport, discusses the Leatt neck brace with Witches skipper Chris Louis.

Injured Witch Mark Loram, back in the Foxhall pits and helping Tobi Kroner.

Marcin Rempala crashes again after getting caught between
Belle Vue Aces' James Wright and Ryan Fisher.

Swindon's Lee
Richardson breaks
down at the start
as (from the left)
Jesper B. Jensen,
Kim Jansson and
Andrew Moore
race away.

Chris Louis inside Adam Shields at Lakeside.

2007 RIDER AVERAGES – ALL OFFICIAL MATCHES
(LEAGUE, CUP & CRAVEN SHIELD)

	M	R	PTS	BP	TOT	CMA	F	P
Chris Louis	38	190	355	20	375	7.89	0	2
Jesper B. Jensen	12	53	86	10	96	7.25	0	0
Robert Miskowiak	37	180	296	11	307	6.82	2	0
Kim Jansson	35	156	199	31	230	5.90	0	0
Tobias Kroner	34	170	208	35	243	5.72	0	0
Zbigniew Suchecki	30	121	106	17	123	4.07	0	0
Marcin Rempala	36	155	129	26	155	4.00	0	0
Chris Schramm	9	40	28	7	35	3.50	0	0

The 2008 Ipswich Witches: (from the left) Jarek Hampel (kneeling), Chris Schramm, Tobi Kroner, Chris Louis, Piotr Swiderski, Robert Miskowiak (kneeling) and Steve Johnston.

Now in his 20th season Chris Louis is coming towards the end of his racing career, but is still a force to be reckoned with, especially around Foxhall. As well as scoring points on the track, Chris is also heavily involved off it, helping father John with promotional duties at the club. When the time does come for him to finally step off the bike, it is expected that he will take over full time promoting of the club.

Date of birth: 9 July 1969
Birthplace: Ipswich, England
Nationality: British

Ipswich career: 1989 – Present

Major honours:
World Under-21 Champion: 1990
World Championship 3rd Place: 1993
British Champion 1998: 2000

2008 starting average: 7.28

Robert Miskowiak

Robert Miskowiak returns to Foxhall Stadium for a fourth successive season. Although his early 2008 scoring has been affected by illness, he is now showing signs of recapturing the form that saw the Pole finish last season with a number of impressive performances.

Date of birth: 21 November 1983
Birthplace: Rawicz, Poland
Nationality: Polish

Ipswich career: 2005 – Present

Major honours:
World Under-21 Champion: 2004

2008 starting average: 6.69

Jarek Hampel

Jarek Hampel returns for his second spell at the club. A Grand Prix regular, Hampel failed to qualify for the series this season, after missing three of the rounds last year because of injury. The Polish star comes back into the side on his 2003 average and is expected to improve on that considerably during the course of the year.

Date of birth: 17 April 1982
Birthplace: Lodz, Poland
Nationality: Polish

Ipswich career: 2000 – 2003, 2008

Major honours:
Polish Under-21 Champion: 2001
World Under-21 Champion: 2003
World Team Champion: 2005, 2007

2008 starting average: 6.27

Steve Johnston returns for his second spell with the club after an 11-year absence. Last season he celebrated success at Coventry, helping them achieve the treble and he has also won a league championship medal with Oxford in 2001.

Date of birth: 12 October 1971
Birthplace: Kalgoorlie, Australia
Nationality: Australian

Ipswich career: 1997, 2008

2008 starting average: 5.41

Piotr Swiderski

Piotr Swiderski joined Ipswich this season on loan from rivals, Peterborough, and has started the year in such fine form that he is currently the club's top averaged rider. If the Pole can keep this form up throughout the year then he will prove to be an extremely shrewd signing for the Suffolk side.

Date of birth: 11 May 1983
Birthplace: Gostyn, Poland
Nationality: Polish

Ipswich career: 2008

2008 starting average: 5.19

Tobi Kroner

Tobi Kroner begins his second full season with the Witches in 2008, after joining the club part way through 2006. The German made rapid strides towards the end of last season and looks to have a promising future in the sport.

Date of birth: 16 October 1985
Birthplace: Dohren, Germany
Nationality: German

Ipswich career: 2006 – Present

2008 starting average: 4.89

Chris Schramm

Chris Schramm has taken the step up to become full time Elite League rider in 2008 after making nine appearances for the club as No. 8 last season.

Date of birth: 30 May 1984
Birthplace: Maldon, England
Nationality: British

Ipswich career: 2007 – Present

2008 starting average: 3.00

Chris Louis in discussion with Jerek Hampel (above) and with
new team manager, Pete Simmons (below).

New signing
Piotr Swiderski
makes a start.

Jarek Hampel

Jarek Hampel leading Jonnas Kylmakorpi of Lakeside.

Chris Louis inside a battling Andreas Jonsson.

Steve Johnston (left), Chris Louis (right) and Andreas Jonsson.

Piotr Swiderski on the inside of Jonsson.

ahp At Heart Ltd Titles

For more information or to buy any of these titles visit www.atheart.co.uk or your local bookseller

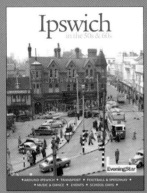

Ipswich in the '50s & '60s

David Kindred brings to life the changing face of Ipswich in the 50s & 60s in this book, using his own collection of outstanding vintage photography, as well as images from the archives of the *Evening Star* and those donated by local residents.

978-1-84547-102-6

£14.99

Ipswich – The War Years

The Second World War affected the lives of all those who were growing up during this turbulent period in world history. This book is a collection of the feelings and memories of numerous Ipswich residents, recounted with the use of some wonderful photography and personal memories of events.

978-1-84547-095-1

£14.99

Lancashire Titles

Pocket Belle Vue	978-1-84547-164-4	£6.99
Manchester At War	978-1-84547-096-8	£14.99
The Changing Face of Manchester Vol. 1 (Revised Edition)	978-1-84547-189-7	£14.99
The Changing Face of Manchester Vol. 2	978-1-84547-104-0	£12.99
The Changing Face of Manchester Vol. 3	978-1-84547-160-6	£12.99
The Changing Face of Manchester in the Seventies	978-1-84547-117-0	£12.99
Around Manchester in the 50s & 60s (Revised Edition)	978-1-84547-192-7	£12.99
	978-1-84547-185-9	£12.99
Manchester City FC: 125 Years of Football	978-1-84547-183-5	£12.99
Lancashire's Four Seasons	978-1-84547-188-0	£12.99
The Ribble Valley in Pictures	978-1-84547-153-8	£12.99
Blackpool Then and Now	978-1-84547-182-8	£12.99
Legends: The great players of Blackpool FC	978-1-84547-136-1	£12.99
Chorley Past	978-1-84547-137-8	£12.99
Garstang Past	978-1-84547-184-2	£12.99
Wigan Past		

Yorkshire Titles

Flooded Yorkshire 2007	978-1-84547-180-4	£14.99
The Great Flood	978-1-84547-150-7	£13.99
The Great South Yorkshire Floods	978-1-84547-178-1	£12.99
Leeds Past	978-1-84547-131-6	£12.99
Scarborough Past	978-1-84547-166-8	£12.99
Yorkshire At War	978-1-84547-109-5	£14.99
Yorkshire Past	978-1-84547-106-4	£14.99
Yorkshire Past: East Riding	978-1-84547-126-2	£12.99
Yorkshire Past: North Riding	978-1-84547-125-5	£12.99
Yorkshire Past: West Riding	978-1-84547-127-9	£12.99
Yorkshire's Picture Post Vol. 1	978-1-84547-097-5	£14.99
Yorkshire's Picture Post Vol. 2	978-1-84547-114-9	£16.99

Sheffield Titles

Bygone Transport: Sheffield on the Move	978-1-84547-100-2	£14.99
Sheffield FC - Celebrating 150 Years	978-1-84547-174-3	£12.99
A Year in the Garden	978-1-84547-105-7	£14.99
Sheffield at Play	978-1-84547-108-8	£14.99

Lincolnshire & Southern Counties Titles

Grantham in the News 1951-1975	978-1-84547-141-5	£12.99
Grantham in the News 1976-2000	978-1-84547-173-6	£12.99
Grantham in Focus	978-1-84547-142-2	£9.95
Mere Quacks	978-1-84547-167-5	£12.99
Skegness Past	978-1-84547-143-9	£14.99
Ipswich in the '50s & '60s	978-1-84547-102-6	£14.99
Ipswich - the War Years	978-1-84547-095-1	£12.99
Ipswich Speedway: A Decade in Pictures	978-1-84547-191-0	£12.99
Spalding Flower Parade: The Golden Years	978-1-84547-159-0	£12.99
Spalding in the Fifties	978-1-84547-158-3	£12.99
Northampton Looking Back Vol. 1	978-1-84547-157-6	£12.99
Northampton Looking Back Vol. 2	978-1-84547-186-6	£12.99
Walking in the Wolds with Hugh Marrows	978-1-84547-144-6	£8.95
Walking Through Lincolnshire's History	978-1-84547-187-3	£8.95
Worksop Past	978-1-84547-149-1	£12.99

Forthcoming Titles

Spalding in the Sixties
Kettering in Pictures
Burnley Legends
The Derbyshire Times Railway Album
Market Harborough in the '70s
Sheffield Wednesday Legends
Sheffield United Legends
Stockport County Legends
Sheffield Star Railway Album
Rochdale AFC Legends

For more information: If you would like any further information on any of the above titles please contact us at the address below.
At Heart Ltd: 32 Stamford Street, Altrincham, Cheshire, WA14 1EY **Tel:** 0161 924 0159 **Fax:** 0161 924 0160